Revenge of Love
Letters of Hope

Revenge of Love
Letters of Hope

Lindsay Shigemoto

Heartseer Press

Published in the United States by Heartseer Press, an imprint of Finn-Phyllis Press, Phoenix, Arizona

Revenge of Love / Lindsay Shigemoto — 1st ed.

Library of Congress Control Number: 2025907182
Paperback ISBN: 979-8-9929588-1-2
eBook ISBN: 979-8-9929588-2-9

Cover design by JetLaunch.net

To the ones who feel unseen

Acknowledgements

To the love of my life, my husband, Steve, who has been all in and supported my journey since we found each other at 15 years old. Thank you for reminding me that dreams really do come true. Thank you for always participating in the shenanigans and listening to my wild ideas. Here's to one wild idea coming to life. I love you beyond even my words can express.

To my children, Kielle and Landon, who inspire me to be better every day. You are the reason for these words of hope, because you are hope, you are love in action, you are beautiful humans. Thank you for teaching me that love has no limits. I love you so much.

To my most beloved friends, Tiffany, and Elizabeth. Thank you for seeing me. Thank you for teaching me how to be loved and deepen my own ability to love. Thank you for speaking the truth. Thank you for never giving up on me. Thank you for the tears, the hugs and the laughter. Oh, my heart, the laughter. My beautiful sisters, you make me better. I love you.

To my soul friend, Jena. Thank you for being on the other end of the conversation when this idea came to life. I am forever grateful our paths have intersected and that our souls found each other. Thank you for being one of my biggest cheerleaders to make this dream come true. You are a world changer. Keep shining your radiant light. I love you.

To my favorite English teacher, Mrs. Weston. Thank you for leading me to find my writing voice. Thank you for investing in your students so deeply. Your quick wit and passion to pull out the author in all of us still lives deep within my being. Thank you for letting that people pleasing young girl do all of the unnecessary extra credit, because you knew it fed my soul to write. I love you.

To Cathy, and Suzanne, for inspiration, encouragement, editing, and your endless support. To Elizabeth at Finn-Phyllis Press for her guidance, patience and expertise throughout the process.

Lastly, but most definitely not least, to my grandpa Loren who left this world far too early. Thank you for teaching me not to quit. Thank you for speaking words of hope and life over me as a young child. And thank you for letting me type stories away on your old typewriter as a teeny tiny child. I hope I have made you proud and worthy of all of those childhood key clicks. I love you.

CONTENTS

Preface

I have seen and experienced far too much hate in my life thus far. The actions of one toward another, awful words spoken between souls, harmful intent, hate. It can be overwhelming.

That's when I decided to do something more. I was chatting with a friend, and I said the phrase "the best revenge is love," and my baby idea was born.

My life legacy project. Revenge of Love. "In a world full of hate, the best revenge is love."

Words matter. Actions matter.

Revenge of Love is just that. Pulling the opposite of all of the hate we experience and conquering it through love. With love.

I began sending words of hope and encouragement to friends many years ago. Through a series of events in 2022 and 2023 this process exploded into something bigger.

What you see on these pages are some of these words. My hope is that one life is touched, sparking something new or rekindling a flame within, causing a ripple effect of love from one soul to another and another.

One soul at a time. Loving deeply. Fiercely. Freely.

If you ever find yourself in the crosshairs of hate or feel the heaviness of the hate that exists in the world; these pages are for you. Be the love in action. Be the revenge. You are what will change this world for the better.

In a world full of hate, the best revenge is love.

Return to Sender

I often speak about words. Words have power. Life sustaining, or weapons of destruction. But what about our own thoughts? The lies, the unwanted visitors, the ones we've rejected many times before.

Why is it that sometimes these thoughts pop back up as we move deeper in growth, and elevate to the next level of our human? Some days they have no power over us, but other days, they take us out.

Some days are full of lies. We have a choice. Accept the lies or return to sender. We are far from perfect. We struggle sometimes. I admit, the lies get me roped in for a little bit sometimes. I get discouraged occasionally, but one thing I am not is a quitter. I've been given time in this world, so I fight. And I encourage you to fight the lies too.

Sometimes our current self is not running the show. It sometimes is a past version of ourselves, scared of rejection when asking for help, scared of being helped, scared of failure, more scared of success, and scared of being seen. They all stem from the same root. Lies- that it isn't worth the fight, that we aren't worth the fight. Straight from the deepest evil. Lies. So far from the truth.

There is no magic key or set recipe for healing and growth. It is rarely a straight line. It isn't called the messy middle because it's lovely. Oh, but we pause, our people whisper truth, hope, and love. Then we begin to regain our bearings. We've been here before. We begin to remember the other side. We begin to find ourselves right side up, the lies silenced by truth once again.

The lies stamped RETURN TO SENDER.

My hope is that when you find yourself in that messy middle, battling the lies, that these words may offer hope, love and truth to help you find your bearings once again. That you remember what you know. That you are a miracle. You have value. You matter. You have a purpose that only you can fulfill. You are so needed in this world.

Metamorphosis

People often speak of butterflies and transformation. How a tiny caterpillar wraps itself up and poof transformed into a beautiful butterfly. We are missing so much of the lesson.

The metamorphosis isn't simple. It isn't pretty. It isn't comfortable. Why do we pretend it is? Why are we so quick to rush to the end result without the messy middle?

The messy middle. That's exactly why. Often, we avoid that part because we want the result without the challenge. We want growth without the pain. We want beauty without discomfort. That's the delusion.

That tiny caterpillar knows it is time to go willingly into the painful messy middle, to be deconstructed from what is familiar in order to transform into the beautiful. In order to grow into the next level, in order to fly free, it must go willingly or die staying the same.

And so must we. Growth is not always comfortable. Growth is not always beautiful. Growth is rarely if ever the "poof" of transformation.

We, just like the caterpillar, have a choice. Stay the same and wither away or go willingly into the messy transformation of growth. What is more painful?

Staying the same, or going through the process with the hope of emerging something we were designed to become?

Innately the caterpillar knows what its next steps are. And so do we. It is deep within us. If you are sitting in the uncomfortable it may just be your time for another metamorphosis.

The butterfly is so much more when we understand the whole process. Even the icky parts. What will you be when you emerge from your chrysalis? What does your next level look like?

What are you waiting for? The world needs you to emerge so you too can fly free.

Breadcrumbs

What do you want to be when you grow up? A question we likely were asked as young children. My son's answer when he was in preschool was, "I want to be an adult because they get to do cool stuff," quite the literal answer, but even then, he understood the opportunities that this world holds for each of us.

The world is often loud, drowning out dreams. Expectations. Direction. Tradition. Submission. And just like that the childhood dream often fades away into a childhood memory and distant dream.

My daughter was always styling, coloring, and often cutting her dolls' hair. The world's influences and other people's opinions and unwanted expectations of what success looked like began...but thankfully we spoke life back into her to follow her passions. It just took some remembering. Unburying the passion. Her breadcrumbs. The days of playing hair salon both with humans and dolls, literal evidence found in childhood boxes. The evidence was clear and little by slow, her dream re-emerged to become her reality.

Do you remember what your dream was as a young child? What was your focus? What was your passion? Where did your imagination take you?

It just takes some remembering of those times before the world became loud. There is no timeline for life. It is never too late to live your dream.

You were created for something special and unique. Something, only you can bring to life in this world.

Find your breadcrumbs

But Hope

Pitch black. Total darkness. The moments just before are always the darkest. In this facade of an empty abyss, we find truth. The truth that our own strength or wisdom will never be enough. It is here where we come to understand and slowly accept that we must depend entirely on hope.

Little by slow, obstacles and senselessness transform into power and wisdom. Hope changes everything. If something is calling you, pursuing you, and pulling you, then perhaps the turning point for you lies within this hope.

Why are we in such a hurry to rush through to the good parts? Is it because devastation and hard times don't fit into our picture of how things ought to be? It doesn't fit into anyone's picture. Yet, challenges are often the path to freedom. To surrender.

We find the ones who show us how to hope beyond the circumstances. It's one thing to predict the future. It's quite another to go through the challenges willingly.

Many will not understand. Some embrace this destiny through faith, don't be fooled…it is never easy. But hope. The promise of hope. It is trust in something

---

Lindsay Shigemoto

better, something more that causes us to wager everything we are. Hope.

When the fear threatens to overwhelm, the lies of self creep in; remember the promise of hope. Hope because we are here. Hope because we love. Hope because we are love. A hope for the next promise. A hope for better. A hope for the next beautiful. A hope for dreams. Hope.

We will find the ones who model hope for us. The ones who have come through the fire. The ones who survived because of hope. The ones who live.

The Revealing

I've walked along the beach many times at low tide in my lifetime. Something was different this time, something new revealed, because I am different.

The low tide unveiling a hidden world of beauty, life and treasures secretly tucked beneath the surface. A revealing as the waves are pulled back.

In life when we pull back defenses, we too are revealed. When we pull back those things that have kept parts of us hidden; we experience an unmasking, a shining, an exposure of beautiful treasures we possess.

The tides come and go in a beautiful dance with the moon. The previously hidden, once again protected; but not forgotten.

Once acknowledged, our hidden talents, passions and purpose can no longer be forgotten. A coordinated dance with creation in the timing of action, but of which these things can no longer be ignored.

In divine choreography, the right people will witness the found beauty and walk alongside us as we journey forward; our humanness moving in synchronicity with our talents, living out our purpose.

The revealing, the exposure, the sacred truths; will always find refuge in the timing of the high tide. As you launch further into your journey, remember to rest; but never rely on being hidden. You are meant to be seen, to be heard, and to be celebrated.

This revealing is yours. Claim it proudly.

What's in Your Bag?

Did you ever play the game what's in your bag at a party or as a child? Over the years, my observations came down to three types of people: the minimalists, the collectors, and the middle of the roads. The minimalist typically has the essentials that any one person would need in a bag. The collectors typically had a Mary Poppins type bag of essentials but either excessive amounts of incidental items; old receipts, trash, random items weighing the bag down or a collection of haphazard but very useful items. The middle of the roads would often have some of the essentials and some of the variety of the collector. The minimalist; a lightweight bag, the middle of the road; begins to get a little heavier, and the non-useful collectors; often carrying around excess weight that often serves no purpose.

Such is the same with our life bags. Are you a minimalist, a collector, or a middle of the road?

What are you carrying with you each day? Love? Compassion? Hope? Faith? Resentment? Burdens? Anger? Are they life giving or are they burdens?

What are you lifting and walking through life with each day? The forgotten receipts of resentment, hidden anger, bitterness all weigh us down without being in the forefront of our minds. They are like wet sand, heavy, burdensome, and not always visible. Little by slow, the weight of these negative items we carry around cause fatigue, pain, and seep into the rest of our bag like a leaky drink ruining our wanted items. Slowly making their presence known and taking over the bulk of our bags. Hope, love, and compassion begin to leak out, get taken out, or fall away because the hidden burdens are no longer hidden, and the wet sand has taken over.

It is easy to get caught in the trap and lie of "don't you know these things are justified!" Maybe so, but I press, how's that working out for you? Pause and take an honest assessment of how the hidden negatives are serving you each day.

Aren't you tired with what is weighing you down? Where can you begin to do the work and what can you let go? It is time my friends. Begin the work to let these things go. Clear out the wet sand to make room for the beauty.

Take each step today and work to replace one thing weighing you down with one life giving thing. Practice this each day, and soon you will be a minimalist or even a collector of life-giving items which seem to make the bag float on its own.

Wake up each morning, and ask yourself, "what's in my bag," and see how your life changes for the better.

Shift the Atmosphere

Everything we do causes a shift in the atmosphere. This world we live in feels heavy and disconsolate. I think many of us will never understand evil or suffering. But in the face of this we find our people.

We find the ones who step up and speak life and love when breathing hurts, the ones who sing when souls cry out in pain, the ones who dance when spirits feel broken, the ones who paint when only darkness is seen.

These are the helpers. These are the life changers. These are the warriors. Even on the days we might not feel it, it is important to remember that someone out there had their life changed because we showed up.

Keep showing up my warrior friends, you are making huge waves.

Freedom

Our bodies hold memories. Every experience we have is physical, emotional, and spiritual. They cannot be separated.

As artists (we are all artists), we experience things deeply. It is part of us. Deeper things creep out. Layers upon layers exposed. Sometimes it takes our breath away. The intensity feels overwhelming, our soul vibrating at such a high resonance that we don't know if we can catch our breath again. We are breaking open. Completely vulnerable. Exposed.

Maybe that is the point. When we are stretched and pushed to new limits in our vulnerability, in this breaking open, something unseen is released. A deeper level of healing. We all know, it hurts like hell. The unspoken re-experienced all over again, broken open, our vulnerability on display in front of others, to others. And for what? For whom?

Freedom.

Freedom for you, freedom for me, freedom for those on the receiving end of our crafts.

Freedom feels different, but it doesn't have to be scary. That is the lie. The lie is that it is scary. The old will try to suck us back into the familiar prison. Doubt whispers of deceit and lies incessantly seeking to regain control. We must stand firm and take each step in new hope and freedom remembering what love is; not only is it good, but mighty and powerful. Love has ALL power. Truth always wins. We must seek and stay in truth every moment of every day. Love is rooting for us, and our freedom.

Freedom: where the lost are found, the hurting are healed, where the warriors emerge, where strength expands, and the love flows freely.

My wish for you is that you always feel true safety, that you only feel pure love and encouragement. That you always feel supported and validated in your journey. That on the hard, vulnerable, and exposed days, you never ever feel alone. We somehow find the people who get it and understand.

I honor your journey. Through the pain, you will find freedom.

Find Your Reason

If today is another challenging day, find your reason.

When you step outside take a deep breath, the kind that goes down to your toes and into every cell. Exhale and release yesterday. Turn your face toward the sun. Even when the sun is covered by clouds, it still shines brightly.

Circumstances of life often cloud our purpose, much like the clouds mask the shining sun. But it still exists, shining brightly behind the facade. Belief in what we know to be true. Belief in experiences and knowing.

Your reason for showing up today might just be hidden in the circumstances. But it is there, it is shining brightly. Just like you.

Trust Your Spot

When things feel out of control, trust your spot. Things can get dark and twisty, and we forget what we know. Gymnasts, divers, and dancers learn to trust their spot. A constant, the stability.

I remember the first day I lost my spot diving. The sky was the same blue as the water, I panicked and lost it. And in the middle of my dive, I bailed. It became dark and twisty. I didn't trust my knowing. I didn't find my way back to it with my rotation count. And I hit that water hard. I pulled my weak body out of the water and felt defeated. The defeat and hopelessness I felt in this moment was probably worse than any physical pain.

When the world feels chest crushingly heavy from reading the news or knowing of suffering, when our circumstances are confusing, when it feels dark and twisty and we can't tell the sky from the water we can lose our spot, our center, our source of focus.

The truth is, we innately know the way back, we innately know how to find it again. But sometimes we need help. Your pure heart will bring you the people. The ones who remind you, the ones who teach you, the ones who encourage and support you. The ones who are love. The ones who are light. Your spot finders.

Our spot finders remind us, help us to remember the feeling, to trust the training we have been through and of the life lessons that we pull from. And then, we pick up our strong, not weak, black and blue bodies and march back up that tall ladder and throw the dive again, trusting our spot even when the blue sky and water match.

Allow yourself to remember, to be encouraged, to refocus on your spot. My wish for you is a complete recharge. You don't have to carry the weight of the world. The love and light you bring forth will do that.

Answer to Prayer

Never think that what you have to give is insignificant. There will always be someone who needs what you offer.

My friend once said, "Someone is praying a prayer waiting on God, and he is waiting on you to be the answer to their prayer."

Sometimes I fight with the gifts. What if the timing isn't right, what if I missed something, what if they aren't received as intended. Then I am gently reminded that I am not that powerful. That is not my responsibility. None of this is up to me. My ONLY responsibility is to ask, receive and share. It is a beautiful thing to hold this space for others. Often, I feel inadequate and undeserving.

On our hard personal days, it sometimes (at least I find) is difficult to believe that I make a difference. That what I do is worth it. These words for others bring up a lot, I imagine I am not the only one. That gut wrenching roundhouse kick to the spirit because of our gifts, on those days, it is really challenging.

I don't have all of the answers. Nor do I want that responsibility. I do know that it absolutely matters. When we do what we have been assigned by something bigger than us to do, we show up no matter how painful. In offering others what they need because of us, something deeper is revealed, healed, and sealed in love within us.

I imagine you too, have been the unknown answer to many people's prayers or hopes through your gifts and talents. Even on the hard days, you know deep within you, the impact is earth shaking.

Keep showing up. Even on the hard days.

Already Enough

You are already enough. The pressure to be more, and do more feels like heavy weights being added with each step.

When we have dreams, we strive to achieve them. We set goals and take steps to achieve those goals. The plan of action for a step closer. But do you know what? Even if things don't go as planned, that does not dictate your worth, your value or your impact.

When we set a target, it is a lesson. A lesson moving us forward or a lesson failed allowing us to reevaluate. If a task is failed, it doesn't mean we are a failure. Again, a failed attempt does not mean we are failures. I am not a failure. You are not a failure. My friend, we are not that powerful. The universe of love will guide us to the whos, the whens and the hows we need. We just need to pay attention.

I want to encourage you, that no matter what happens in this life, you are not a failure, you are already enough. The universe will bring forth the people, places and things for your growth and movement. There is no judgment or condemnation in growth. That is not love. Love supports, encourages, and walks alongside cheering you no matter what. And when you are down, it reaches a hand to say that's okay, we can sit here for a moment and then carries you when you can't get up on your own. Love expects nothing, it accepts that you are already enough. And love will stand with you as you take another brave step forward.

Masterpiece of Your Soul

When the words wouldn't flow, I painted. There is something about the arts that cannot be explained or rationalized. Because it is pure. It is deep from within. The brokenness of the world cannot stop the healing powers of art. Every pirouette, every leap, every paint stroke, every melody, every poetic word is protected. Because these things are Freedom, these are Life, these are Love. There have been many times throughout my life when I lost my way and couldn't find the words for a page, the vision for a canvas, or the inspiration for the choreography. Have you ever felt like that? I'm guessing yes, us pure hearted tend to.

Inspiration is hard some days when humanness- the human mess is so heavy. When the bricks on our chests leave us gasping for air as the world tries to bury the passion, we close our eyes and remember. We remember the good. We get back up and we take the first move to dance a step, write a word, paint a line. The beauty within art is so powerful. So today, do it for yourself. Paint, write, or dance for that thing deep within you. Do this in harmony with your spirit. The release of a pure innocent thing of beauty into a harsh world will transcend deeply. You are worthy of your own beautiful masterpiece.

Shine Bright with Purpose

The world needs more of you. You are not expendable. You are not incidental. You are not replaceable. I remember a time when if I had heard these words, I wouldn't be able to comprehend or integrate them. I hardly recognize that version of me now, and I honor the hard work she did to get me to where I am today.

These words are valid. These words are truth.

Some days are more challenging than others. Lies from the past try to draw us back, the world feels heavy, situations feel irreparable, and none of these things negate these words. No matter what is happening to us, or around us, we have to remember these truths.

Sometimes we need reminders of these truths. That we shouldn't shrink back, that we should shine our brightest, we are valuable, and we are on purpose, with a purpose.

The people who say otherwise are not meant for us. Our people will celebrate our successes, encourage our radiant light and will walk into uncharted territory with us. They will never ask you to dim your light, cast you aside, or make you feel less than the powerful warrior that you are.

Now go conquer this day and let's shine some light into this broken world.

Receive

When we suffer hardship or are coming through a dark time in our lives, most of the time our confidence is wearing thin. Acute stress, chronic stress or any kind of tragedy or heartache really takes a toll on our confidence. It breaks down our psychological defenses and can sometimes create a hope or faith crisis.

I find myself asking more "why" and lack of hope questions, in these times. When hope feels so far away and unfamiliar a thing. The "Why did this happen? How can anything good come out of this?" Our emotional confusion can distort our spiritual perception. A grief fog, or heaviness can cut us off from being able to see clearly. Coping with emotional pain requires so much energy.

I often wonder if this is why whatever is bigger than us gives us people who know and feel along with us, just somehow knowing and carrying the load of pain and heartache along with us.

We can take time to care for our tender hearts and reposition ourselves. To ask for what we need, to regain our bearings and get our stability back.

When we are healing from deep heartache, from wounds, there are times when our emotions are going to strive to dictate our choices and drive discouragement. Sometimes rather than letting our emotions rule the roost, we have to dethrone them and pull in what we know to be true. It forces our soul, our mind and our emotions to yield to our human spirit that is in alignment with whatever is bigger than us.

The dark and twisties or purple swirlies where faith and feelings are at battle with the lies that we aren't good enough, that we are failures; but where faith says, the universe always acts in our good. When the lies say, we aren't safe, the universe and faith say, look who I have sent your way. When our doubt says, our scars and wounds limit us for life, faith says we are useful not in spite of our scars but BECAUSE of them.

Our scars, our wounds, our grief and our heartache are difficult to bear but they do not determine our future, nor do they define us. Instead, they are opportunities to experience another layer of the universe's loving presence and to launch us into a deeper universal understanding of this immeasurable love.

Draw in that love, that understanding. It's all around us. The answers and healing will come. They always do. It's okay to be seen. It's okay to be loved. It's okay to be vulnerable. It's okay because we are never alone. Never ever.

Light Wins

The darkness has too many unknowns. The literal and figurative darkness. Here's what I have learned. Light wins in both. Always.

When we bring a source of light into the dark the threat of the unknown lessens. Even in dark valleys, light hits. When we bring light into the darkness we begin to see shadows. Shadows aren't to be feared; they simply cannot exist without a source of light. They just can't. They rely on light.

When things feel dark around us, just like a night-light is a solution, so here light is the solution. Sometimes we have to search for a light source. Sometimes within ourselves, sometimes we draw on others for their light. The beautiful thing about light is that it cannot be contained. It radiates, it spreads, it casts out darkness.

Shine radiantly. Be the light for someone else today. Let someone shine brightly for you. My hope for you today is that you find a source of light to carry you through this day and every other day.

Love Root

I think of my favorite tree. She is worn and weathered. She has seen many storms, but she stands strong. Despite everything that has happened to her, her roots run deep. Some see a broken dying tree. I see something more alive because she is fierce. A protector. A nurturer. And I love her. I'm convinced that she survives, because her deep roots are love. She is grounded in love. She provides in love. Oh, how I long to be as fiercely loving as this tree, and I only allow people into my life who remind me of this tree.

My hope for you is that you can tap into both your own deep roots of love and into those who surround you in life. On the hard days, heck even on the great days; my hope for you is that you can find rest and comfort. Allow yourself to be fiercely loved. There is no expectation or agenda with deeply rooted love. It just is. It just is.

Crunchy Water

I often give my ginormous Golden Retriever, Pickles, his favorite special snack of "crunchy water" AKA ice. He hears the words "crunchy water" and will drop whatever he is doing and come and wait. Something so simple, and yet, his tippy tappy feet, circle tail wags, and big, beautiful eyes cannot contain his excitement. This is dog joy.

I hope you find this kind of joy today. It doesn't have to be a huge experience; something so simple, so common, yet everything within you gets excited at the thought of it.

You deserve to take a moment, or many moments for yourself. You are more than a job, more than a performance. Yes, show up as you are able, but do not neglect yourself. Sometimes we forget this piece. You are worthy of all of the crunchy water joy today and every day.

Just Be

I've always been drawn to water, especially the ocean. I savor how something so vast can be both gentle and fierce.

When on vacation growing up, I would spend hours on the beach. Just existing. Appreciating the beauty before me. No expectations, no performance. I could just be.

The gentle waves crashing against my tiny, yet strong frame turn into big crashing waves. The pain I released in those salty tears mixing with the salt water of the ocean was carried out far away from me. Dissipating so nothing else would ever feel their burden.

In this life, I long to be like the ocean. Gentle, yet fierce, intimate, yet vast, and a safe healing place for many. Accepting the tears and stories is a privilege, never a burden. I stand in gratitude for the ones who I have the honor of loving in this life. The ones who need an ocean of a friend.

My wish for you today is that you sit and imagine yourself on a warm sandy beach, the gentle waves lapping at your feet, and you release what you have been carrying. It's heavy. It's okay, the ocean will take it far far away with its crashing waves. Returning only beauty, comfort and love. Refreshing restoration to

Lindsay Shigemoto

your whole body, mind and spirit. You are going to be
okay. Never alone. Never ever.

Just be.

Life Unfinished

When I was a little girl, I loved carousel horses. I wanted my very own, but not ANY carousel horse, I wanted an original, so I asked my dad to make me one. I was probably 4 years old. When I was 18, we picked out the design and he began the planning and preparation for this project. When I was 22, he began the physical task of making the horse.

My dad was a very intelligent man and worked very hard at his job, but anyone who knew him would tell you that his employment was not his passion. He loved fly fishing (especially tying flies), gourmet cooking, and woodworking. And I am not exaggerating when I say, he was a master at these three things. He was a master, because he LOVED creating.

The day came and he began piecing the wood together, gluing, sanding, and carving my horse. I dreamed about how we would paint it, where I would place it in my house and how I would cherish that piece I had waited nearly my whole life to be completed. Many other projects came and went in between, and my dad would work on the horse a little bit here, a little bit there.

Many hours were spent, measuring, cutting, gluing, clamping pieces together with immense amounts of pressure. Followed by sanding, carving, and blowing away the unnecessary sawdust. Then more sanding, carving, and blowing. Slowly, out of these blocks of wood, we began to see the emerging beauty of a carousel horse. Constant work, constant pressure, carving and sanding away the unnecessary to create what the master intended.

We are given a life, and it isn't instantly perfect and beautiful. We experience times of being measured up to self-imposed or other imposed standards, periods of extreme pressure, painful carving and sanding away at the basic form of our existence. Oftentimes a quite excruciating process, and oftentimes it feels hopeless, but something never gives up on us. Delicately and lovingly giving us what and who we need to make us more beautiful souls. The gentle blow of breath to clear the sawdust of the painful process to reveal the perfectly detailed line that will soon become a pivotal piece of our journey.

We are never finished being worked on; it is truly a lifelong process. We get the tools we need to become the beautiful soul we were intended to be, but we must be willing to withstand the pressure and pain.

My dad died in 2009. His tools and creations sit still in his workspace. Unfinished projects all around, but frozen in time on the way to beauty.

Today, I see a more beautiful life lesson than any completed carousel horse anyone could ever create. A project unfinished, much like all of us, until our purpose here is complete. I hope you remember in the refining process that; you are not forgotten; you are being prepared for even more beauty. You are so very loved, you are so very important, and you, like the unfinished carousel horse, have a very important message that only you as an individual can share with the world.

The Journey

When we look back to the situations, the people, the everything that brought us to the right here, right now, we gain new perspectives of our journey.

Sometimes we are taken on a journey or many that we didn't have planned, and we didn't know we needed. We arrive in a place in the next phase of preparation for everything we dream.

Sometimes we take detours and run the universe's red lights, but if we are willing, we are gently redirected to the path beautifully designed for us. And often it doesn't look like what we had planned, or even what is right in front of us.

It might not and often doesn't make sense to our rational brains. It isn't until we look back and see the beautiful set up. Sometimes the interruption of our plans redirects us to our purpose.

Finding gratitude in the no, in the not right now, in the disappointments, in the seeming blindsides of change or discovery, in the pause. Challenging times breed hope. The perfect setup for where we are going. The hope of something more.

Lindsay Shigemoto

Through the redirections, heartbreak and challeng-
ing times, perseverance builds character, and character
builds hope. A hope that breeds change. An elevation
in the perfect setup for our dreams.

Your strength of character breeds hope. Hope for
you, hope for humanity. Your life and path are beauti-
ful. In both challenging and good times, those who see
and love you will stand firm by your side.

Sandpaper Angels

When I lay my head down on my pillow at night, I ask, "let me be treated by others tomorrow, how I treated others today." It isn't to be feared; it's actually working out pretty well. When I love well, I am left to love even better the next day.

Everything is a teacher. The tug of war between good and evil, light and dark, the kindhearted and the bullies.

I was once asked who my teachers were. I answered, "the people I want to be like." I was offered an additional perspective. While yes, these people are definitely our biggest teachers, who we surround ourselves with, who we want to emulate; there are other teachers we need to acknowledge. The ones who rub us the wrong way, the ones who have behaviors we find offensive and the ones we sometimes think are just plain awful, our bullies. I call these, the sandpaper angels.

These sandpaper angels teach us too. I look at the behavior or action I find offensive. I ask myself why don't I like this, what about their actions bother me? Once I identify it, I make note of exactly what I didn't

Lindsay Shigemoto

like, take an internal inventory and strive to never treat someone that way, or do that action.

These people teach us exactly what we don't want to be like, how we don't want to behave, what we don't want to be known or remembered for. I have had many sandpaper angel lessons in my lifetime. I am not going to lie, I still get hurt too. The difference now is, I know what is me and what is not mine to own. I'm thankful for the ability to say no thank you to the ick, integrate what is of value, and walk away with new knowledge of what and how not to be in this life.

May I treat others so well today, that tomorrow I can love even harder.

I hope you have a day with few sandpaper angels and are only surrounded by encouraging beauty today.

Release

When we hold in how we truly feel we silence our truth. We create inner sickness and turmoil. Everyone deserves to be heard. Everyone deserves a voice.

Sometimes we just need someone to remind us. Our truth, our thoughts, our pain, our hopes, our dreams, our passions, all matter. They hold so much value. We were never meant to be silent. We were created as an expression of love. And love listens. Love holds space. Love encourages. Love never judges. And honest love is unconditional. No expectations, no judgments, no conforming.

Trust can be such a loaded word. I know the hesitancy in trusting. We often keep people at arm's length. And once in a while we see a similar soul. The ones who know. They are rare, and they are treasures.

Fear may tell us to be quiet. Stay silent. It isn't real. The anxiety, the panic, the feeling of nausea, but then we trust what the universe brought to us. It is in this trusting that we become seen. We all have stories to tell. Stories of impact. With the release, those spaces will only be filled back up with love. Though it may feel hard, or maybe that it won't ever happen, it is your time. Time to release. You won't be alone.

Weeds Masquerading as Flowers

I love people, I know a lot of people and have always made friends easily. With that comes relationships. Sometimes good, sometimes not. I didn't know I had a choice who enters my space until I was free from things of my past. As I got older, I began to think of my relationships as a garden. A beautiful friendship garden. Each flower, unique and full of beauty. After freedom, I began to feel held back and used by some people, sadly, many people. I had to break free. So, I asked, "Please remove the weeds from my garden."

Suddenly people began to fall away as I took some steps back. The ones who took advantage, the ones who I allowed to take advantage, the ones who were actually really mean, and the ones who continued the cycle of abuse in my life. And I felt lighter, and I could breathe. Things continued to get better, but there were things holding me back, preventing me from being my best self. I knew what I needed to do, as painful as it was going to be. I asked, "Please remove the weeds masquerading as flowers."

This process was P.A.I.N.F.U.L. (did I emphasize that enough?) Some relationships had to go, the shadow manipulation, the passive narcissism, ones I once loved deeply, but who I allowed their hurtful behaviors. And then I could see that a lot of it wasn't love at all. As gross as it was, it still hurt to let them go. I asked for the cleansing, so I had to let them go. It is okay for me to miss the good things about them, but in my freedom, I finally realized I can only allow pure hearted souls in my space. I believe people can change, I really do, and maybe one day some of these people might find their way to be planted again. I offer so much grace; the difference now is that I can see deeply and just know the authenticity within someone. This is when I decided that only love warrior tree vibes are allowed.

Let me tell you, the moment I cleared the weeds masquerading as flowers was the moment, the universe opened up room for the most tender-hearted people in my life. I still meet and know a lot of people. The difference now is that only the good ones get planted and grow alongside me.

Some have been here for years, some new. All so worthy of their place in this beautiful friend garden. When the universe brings them, I am so grateful. I often feel inadequate. Each offering something so relevant, so necessary, so pure and deserving of love so they can flourish. I hope I can be a solid life giving, love filled, hope exploding friend they all deserve in this life.

My wish for you is that you see your worth, your value, and that your weeds masquerading as flowers will slowly fade away, so you are surrounded only by such beautiful life-giving friends, that a day doesn't go by that you aren't embraced by love and light. You are worthy. You are loved. You matter. You are valuable. May you find the friend garden where you have the freedom to flourish and grow without limitations.

Justice

Many people never get their justice. The legal kind anyway. So many things deserve justice, but it isn't always a part of the story. Many often escape while waiting.

Running, leaving the grief somewhere on the road. Flying through the air, leaving a part of the brokenness suspended. Always seeking ways to change how things are felt. Adrenaline, the rush, outside input never bringing justice.

Everyone deserves justice. It just might not look like what we think it should look like. Sometimes the universe sorts this out for us. We don't get to decide. This takes a lot of letting go.

Sometimes justice looks like art. The dance, the words, the painting. Somewhere hidden in these things is our story. Our connected souls see it, without ever saying a word, they know. We just know.

Sometimes justice looks like putting pen to paper and telling the truth. Sometimes justice looks like being a loving human who wasn't broken. Sometimes justice looks like taking a stand against another's injustice. Sometimes justice looks like fighting for change.

Lindsay Shigemoto

Sometimes justice looks like shining a light on the hidden.

Turns out, we get our justice. It just looks a little different from what we imagined. Turns out this thing bigger than us never failed us. Turns out, it works in perfect alignment as we find our soul connections, and these are the ones we stand and fight for justice with.

For today, let's fight for justice with our passions. A little more light shining into the darkness, exposing what was never meant to be. Today, someone will feel like they have justice because we show up.

Magic

I love to love people. I love to give freely, because it is who I am.

I love to create for others. As I prepare to create a piece of art, a gift, a meal, whatever the case may be at the time, I begin the process of gathering the tools, the paint, the ingredients and sit in gratitude for the intended recipient. I thank the universe for them, I think about all of the things I love and admire about them, I speak blessings over them. I hope for their peace, their dreams, and for them to always feel loved.

I have been told that I have magic in me. In my hugs, in my hands that create, in my words. It is not magic. It is love.

It really isn't about me at all. I do this in everything I create for someone. I have been given gifts and talents, like we all have, that aren't mine to keep. They are meant to be spread. Every word, every paint stroke, every meal, every full body soul hug I give release love and light to the person on the receiving end. Every time I write a word, paint an image, create the whatever; the thoughts, gratitude and love I have for that person propel the end result.

Your gifts and talents are bringing hope. It is not just a series of seemingly incongruous movements or actions. Even though you might not feel it, you release something into this world full of love and light. Even when it feels just like a series of motions, your soul cannot be stopped. Your spirit isn't quiet. Our minds are tricky, so I am here to remind you that you too are magic. And that magic is love.

My hope for you today and truly every single day, is that you are surrounded by the people in your life that give you hope. That give you life. That help you feel love. That make you feel like there is something magical. Just as you release beauty, love and light into this world with your passions, I hope you believe that YOU ARE WORTHY to receive these things back to you in even more abundance.

Hope for a Better Day

I am learning that I am not in charge of timing.

There will be hard days. Many times, we will isolate ourselves. In these moments we may find ourselves sending encouragement to others, we need for ourselves. The ones we know may also be struggling. No expectations. Checking on those we love, so no one ever feels alone.

It's okay for us to have hard days. As an empath it hurts when we can't help. Goodness, it hurts. And some days it hurts for ourselves and even more because so many others are also hurting.

I'm reminded of Desmond Doss who as he was saving soldiers from both sides in WWII prayed to help just one more, again and again.

So, we stand and humbly ask whatever is bigger than us, today and every day, "Please let me help one more. Just one more."

I hope you never feel alone. That you always have a safe place. To laugh, to cry, to hold space, to celebrate, and to sit silently. Never alone. Never ever.

Celebrate

Every day, I love celebrating the big wins, the little successes (is that even a thing?) and everything in between. Our impact is based on the actions we take and how we leave others feeling when we leave.

In a world full of challenges, perceptions of failure and much disagreement among humans, where do we focus? What do we do with our gifts, with our time here, what legacy are we leaving? In a world full of negative what ifs, and the what ifs of failure…what if we shift the focus.

We need to remind ourselves of the successes. What if someone has hope. What if they decided to stay another day. What if they felt loved for the first time. What if they felt like they mattered. What if they felt represented. What if they felt seen. What if because of us they saw a spark of light. What if they now have just enough hope to continue.

We trust that each day, whatever and wherever the series of seemingly random events take us, we end up exactly where we are supposed to be. Whatever is bigger than us is using us to help others break free from lies, from old ways of thinking and to be an inspiration of hope, and of goodness. It's okay for us to show up and never know the end result of our impact.

As you go through your day, trust that you are exactly where you need to be simply by showing up EXACTLY as you are.

Today will be awesome because you exist.

The Wall

We often use the idiom "hit the wall" to describe when we feel we can't push through, feel depleted, or feel stuck.

In sports we use this to describe the moment we feel like our bodies can't push through physically in training, or for a few more miles. It's not so different when we feel we have a mental or spiritual wall.

There are times when we somehow find the strength to push through- finish the race, finish the training sets, finish a work item, but dang it if pushing through in personal growth sometimes it feels harder.

What if the wall wasn't meant to be something to be pushed through immediately? What if the wall comes up as a place meant for us to lean into and rest for a moment. A place to rest, regroup, evaluate, reassess and plan.

Walls can hold the weight of our resting/pausing. In fact, they can hold many of us who have hit it together or at the same time. A place for others to join in our rest. A place of support, a place to lean on the ones who walk this life journey with us. Walls don't have to mean solitude.

Walls don't mean barricades. Once we are rested and refueled, we get to continue on. Whether it's a wall we climb over, and those who support us will boost us over and climb over with us, or whether it's a wall meant to be broken down, those same people on our journey rally and knock it over or demolish it with us.

Our life journey isn't meant to be solitary. We were made as relational creatures. Of course we need our daily quiet recharges, but that's different. Take time to remind yourself that it's okay to have support and allow people to be on the journey with you. Sometimes old independent habits try to come around again.

The wall is never the end. Nothing is too big to conquer once we rest and take another look. We rest. We recharge. And we go over or through this proverbial wall for the next leg of our journey. We haven't finished here yet.

Lighthouse

I've had many make the analogy of my life impact to a lighthouse. A light that reaches many, a guiding light to safety. It exists to help.

Lighthouses typically symbolize hope and security, safety, and strength and resilience. My goodness, if my life can be one, even just one of those things for someone else or for many, then I hope I live up to that.

Hope and security, the beacon of light piercing through the darkness guiding others to safe passage. The knowing that comes with seeing that light that one will be guided to refuge.

Safety, not only offering shelter during a storm but guiding vessels to the safety that comes with the above hope.

Strength and Resilience, built to withstand some of the earth's harshest storms and remain standing. Never faltering, never destroyed from its purpose.

We will never know all of the lives we reach shining for others. The lights will continue to burn brightly through those we have touched, guided to safety, restored hope and offered refuge. Our legacies, much like the lighthouses, will long outlast us in this world.

And there's nothing extra to do. We shine brightly even in the darkest days, with a reach far beyond our imaginations.

There's nothing you must do other than show up exactly as you are. You are enough. You are valued. You are valuable. You are important.

It's Already in You

Our passions are what we work hard at. What we are gifted to do. Our purpose is WHY we do it. We are taught to "discover our passions, discover our purpose." I thought this meant finding something outside of me. Absolutely not. These things are already in us. They were planted in us at creation. Sometimes the world buries these things with trauma, addictions, and expectations. But we uncover, we dig deep. We keep digging. We keep uncovering. It's the only way to be our truest version of the self we were when we were created.

Clues are planted for us along the way. We often don't know to look for them until after the hard work of digging out of the black tar placed on us.

You know your passions. You are elevating. You know your purpose. You are exploding. We all can feel lost or confused at times. If you feel confusion or doubt, that's not you, that's the world. Close your eyes and remember. You already know, it's already in you. And in those moments of doubt or confusion your love tribe will help remind you of what you already know. In those moments of remembering, they will celebrate with you.

Lindsay Shigemoto

That's what love does. Love is an action word. That is our purpose.

Abundant Love

When we sit in confusion or challenging circumstances are we willing to believe that regardless of what we are experiencing in life, that we are loved deeply? Are we willing to believe that what we are experiencing may be another tool used to draw us closer to others? To our purpose?

That although bad and difficult things happen, those may be the things used as hope we offer to others BECAUSE we survived? Are we willing to accept that sufficient grace is designed specifically for us during times of struggle and hardship?

Are we willing to believe that we don't have to be or do anything to be loved? That simply by existing we are worthy? That we are enough?

Today, will we be willing to see that what is right in front of us is proof of the abundant love for us? Our precious friends, those we call family, our beloved fur babies? That these are the things that represent goodness in an often dark and heavy world?

Mindset for the day, let us see the things right in front of us universally as proof of the abundant love for us. Let us focus on these things, not what we don't have or what we can't fix. Let us appreciate and celebrate what goodness has been given to us in these moments.

That you absolutely are enough in your humanness. Not what you do, have done or will do. That because you exist, that is enough.

Why Not?

Years ago, I had just gone to a retreat up at Lake Tahoe. I heard a lot of good things. Took the things that resonated and left the rest that weren't meant for me. I heard three people share something similar that resonated with me. And I left thinking, why not me?

As I drove home, I became increasingly angry, upset and kept wondering why isn't my situation like this? What is wrong with me? Am I as invalid and undeserving as I grew up believing?

I pulled over to a waterfall spot on my drive home. And as I sat in that beautiful spot I asked "Why Not Me" with all of the sadness and grief coming up again. At some point it has to end. And I had the thought, "why not?" As I thought about this, why don't I believe I'm worth the healing and restoration that I have been working so hard to feel. Then it hit me. I was blocking myself. What was I afraid of? I was afraid of freedom. I was so fearful of freedom that I kept myself in the mental prison of my past. It was routine. It was consistent. It gave a false sense of safety. It was familiar. It was uncomfortably comfortable. I was afraid of moving forward. I was afraid of being successful.

After years of hard work to heal, it came down to this. I sat at that waterfall and let it go. A million things lifted. And I cried. I finally had forgiven myself for things that weren't my fault. Things that were. And I knew I was going to be okay. I continue my healing and growth journey, but had I not let go at this moment, I wouldn't be who I am right now. I wouldn't have the opportunities I have now. I wouldn't know the precious ones I know now. In this moment I believed I was worth it.

Take a deep breath and ask yourself "why not me?" There is SO MUCH goodness that you deserve in this life, waiting for you. You are worthy of it all.

Find the Delights

Have you ever noticed that we see what we are looking for? People buy a new car, and they begin to see that same color, make, and model car everywhere. New puppy? Puppies everywhere! The opposite is also true. Red light? Red lights everywhere. Delayed flight? Suddenly we only see delayed flights on the board.

What if we seek out delights everywhere instead? Beauty? Love? It is already out there. The universe has dispersed these things freely for us. The smile on a stranger's face, the intricacies of the plants we see on our walks, the vast, yet intimate beauty of the sky. Once we begin to seek the delights in the seemingly mundane, our world explodes in a fiery passion for the universe's gifts.

That's how I want to live: a witness to the gifts all around us. Even on the hard days. Even in the routine day to day things, because they are not routine at all. They are each an expression of intimate love and creation.

Let's seek to continually live in appreciation and gratitude so we can be the human expression of the love, light and hope that we know exists. Let us continue to be open vessels for the universe, so when someone sees us, they in turn see the delights of the universe.

One soul at a time, together, we will plant seeds of hope, love and light and be the reason others seek delight.

Naïveté

I've been called many things in my life. Naive is one that continues to be a label given to me.

For many years, I played into that label. It was easier to hide. Play the innocent, doe eyed role. But believe me, I was and am anything but naive. It was an easy label to hide behind, though the lessons I learned from others, actions far outweighed this empty label assigned to me.

I am anything but naive. As an adult, what people now see as naive, is my hope in goodness. I still believe people are innately good and born with love. I believe this because many escape things they were taught- in fact, many are quite literally everything others taught them wasn't acceptable, the opposite of what they tried to make them become. Love won. Some people get lost in this world. I've said it before; I don't understand hate. I refuse to see the world through the lens of hate. I choose to see the world through the lens I was given at creation for this world. Love. Hope. Acceptance. Beauty.

If believing in good, being a believer in better, looks like naïveté to some, that's not my label to carry or play into anymore.

Let's conquer this label-filled world believing in the goodness, the hope, the belief in better, the belief that love transcends all of the evil around. The belief that we can and are making a difference every single day. That we matter. That no matter the distorted lessons thrown at us, no matter what labels, naive or otherwise, have been placed upon us by others or self, that one of only ones that matters is being a vessel of universal love.

Go be a beautiful vessel of this goodness, the better, the love; just by being you. No labels. No expectations. No agenda. Just existence.

Our Past is a Place of Reference Not Residence

The moment I realized I am not defined by what has been done to me, what I have done, the feelings of good enough, not good enough, nor the in between was a day of freedom.

What matters in this life is that we are designed by love that is singing and breathing life into us. Love. Gently nudging us to be who we were created to be.

The darkness of this world will try to draw us back to the past. Whispering the familiar lies. But love does not reside there. And so, I acknowledge my past, I do not excuse what was done, but am grateful for surviving, because as some say, we are still here and that's a freaking miracle.

We surround ourselves with the people who inspire, who teach, who hope. Who reach out a hand when we are stuck in things of the past and who walk alongside us helping us to be brought back to truth, to now. Who remind us we don't live in the "what was" anymore. Who have no agenda other than love.

You are enough. You are life. You are love. You are alive with purpose. And you have a big, beautiful purpose.

The Pause and Rest

Goal setting. Going for it. Stretching. Facing fear. Living your purpose. Unlocking your gifts. All of the be more, do more. The pressure. Oh, the pressure.

But what happens when you get to that point where you are so frustrated that you want to quit? That you want to give up.

We ALL get to that point. The difference between those who ultimately succeed and those who do not, is not how well they handle the success, the progress and the good times. True success is created in moments of doubt, frustration, fear and wanting to give up.

Why?

Because in each moment we have a choice. The choice about what something means and then what we will choose to do as a result. We control our actions and our meanings.

You see, we have no idea what's just on the other side. We have no idea what miracles await us on the other side of not giving up.

To push ourselves, to grow, to really be with the imperfect and courageous action that it takes to grow... that is the real work we must focus on.

So, instead of giving up... I have another idea.

Pause for an hour. Pause for half a day.

Let off some steam. Take the pressure off. Rest. And don't let a temporary moment of frustration, overwhelm or doubt turn into a lifetime of regret.

Micro-rests are great. They allow us to express our frustration, not react, and get back into emotional and spiritual alignment. We come back stronger. We come back to experience the next. We come back to what and where we need to be to experience the next miracle, the next dream.

Give yourself permission to rest. In the middle of it all. It's okay to recenter, to reset, to refocus and realign. You are worth it. You are worth remembering. Not because of anything you must do, simply because you exist. You are a beautiful human so worthy of the goodness ahead.

Truth and Lies

I've been remembering a Bible story I learned many years ago about the woman with the issue of blood. Bleeding for 12 years with no resolution. Imagine having people yell at you "unclean" when you pass by people avoiding you for fear of becoming unclean.

What I've learned from this is what is valuable. All those years of lies being thrown at her—unclean, being made to feel less than, the outcast. Oh, how her heart and soul must have felt. It pains me now to imagine. I relate to the woman in this story. Deeply. The lies and words thrown at me like swords, still screaming loudly at me some days. Trying to pull me back into the dark abyss. I don't live there anymore. I work hard to stay present in truth. But some days the pressure, the lies, the hate tries to pull us back.

In the story, the woman receives her miraculous healing. In ours it looks different. No touch of the garment moments here. It took us deciding to show up for ourselves. Deciding to heal. Deciding to fight to break through these lies. Deciding to dig deep and uproot those very lies that bound us to that old pain. So unfamiliar now, an unwanted enemy that pops in, often in disguise, to try to lure us back. Masquerading as something new. Why? Why are we the target?

Because we are light. Because we are love. Because our purpose is bigger than the darkness. We will face opposition and haters, but we've come through worse.

We focus on the love. We focus on the truths spoken to us. We know the difference. We choose what to believe. The universe brings people who remind us. We find ones who believe for us. We feel the truth. And we trust. Every version of yourself is so proud of how far you have come.

Your hope is believable. Your hope encourages. Your hope heals. Do NOT let the voices of doubt enter in. Combat them with the truth.

To Love and Be Loved

My best friend and I have this tattoo. The Wizard of Oz ruby slippers with the words "To love and be loved" encircling them. A reminder that we are never ever alone.

When I welcome people into my life I do so with no expectations. They are free to be loved deeply. Offered a safe place of love, of healing, of self. No armor. No masks. It takes time for some to understand a space like this.

Loving people is my life force. I was made this way on purpose for this purpose.

The most beautiful things happen authentically. Everyone gets what they need. Loving people deeply is the highest form of connectivity to the universe. Allowing ourselves to be loved this way is a whole other layer. Receiving what we offer. To be loved.

I've found that most people don't know this kind of love. As one whose only purpose is to love this way, it hurt deeply to discover this. I won't accept this as how the world works. I passionately want to change this. So, I ask myself, what's my role? Love. Always love. One by one.

Love is bigger than anything else. It doesn't mean these other things, the struggles, the hard times, aren't real, or invalid; however, love conquers ALL. I was reminded that the few days I felt like I lost myself last week, that my love was still felt. A few knew my dark and twisty status, but the love still prevailed I'm told.

What restores my faith in humanity? Is seeing people be love. Love in human form. What especially makes my heart explode? Watching people realize they ARE love. All I do is show them they are loved freely and unconditionally.

You are love. You are loved. Unconditionally. Unreservedly. Unwaveringly. Unendingly. Because you are enough exactly as you are. A beautiful human with a magical pure soul, exploding ripples of hope every single day.

Love and Math

Math is constant. The answers exist across all nations. Various methods are used to get to the answer, but they all lead to the one answer. 1+1=2. It has always existed.

Love is constant. Love exists across all nations. Various methods are used to express love, but they all lead to the one feeling. It has always existed.

Love and math. Two things that know no barriers. The end result is always the same. Two seemingly unrelated things so intricately intertwined.

Love is exponential. When we love it begins a new equation. We love one soul, that soul in turn loves another, who loves another, and so on. Each soul loving more souls. Increasing in quantity over time.

So, when it seems like loving one more isn't enough, may we remember the big picture of the future. We cannot begin to understand the growth or impact because of the one. Each individual one is an explosion of change. An explosion of love growth.

If we only had the ability to have the birds eye view of this impact. To see every life touched as a result of our love toward another. Maybe we aren't allowed this privilege until our time in this world is finished, for whatever reason.

There is no such thing as too much love. There is no such thing as too big of an impact. Love is our purpose. Only love. Deep, relentless love.

Obstacle Course

Do you ever feel like you have to be on? People get it twisted and think we don't struggle?

Life is a marathon not a sprint, they say…I call the bluff. Most days it feels like some ever-changing obstacle course. And there is no finish line. Like some M.C. Escher inspired nonsense.

There is no need to "arrive." Showing up messy is okay. Showing up with the purple swirlies or dark and twisties is okay. So long as we fight with everything deep within us through that obstacle because there is such beauty ahead.

We might only see the next challenge or be so thick in the mud we can't see the place of rest, but we keep moving. There are no competitors. Only teammates.

Those who get dirty in the mud with us and say, "hey we can stay here for a moment but there's something better just on the other side." The ones who won't leave us behind or make us speed up. The ones who stand or sit or lay with us right where we are. The truth tellers. The encouragers. The ones who have been or are going through it. The real ones.

Not the performers of life. Our obstacle comrades. It takes a team. We learn. Many of us fought so hard alone for so long, letting people in is a battle we fight every day. The, "I got this don't you know?" Well, you know….I don't have it. None of us do. That is a huge obstacle in many of our life races.

No need to perform. No need to be anything that anyone else expects. I don't expect anyone to show up other than how they really are, so why do we place these burdens upon ourselves? It's like throwing obstacles in our own way.

Show up messy. Show up exactly as you are. Those who love you don't expect differently. Those who do are not your people. Do the hard work of remembering the truth. Believe the people reminding you of the truth. Your spirit and soul know. We just need a little remembering.

The purple swirlies and dark and twisties will pass. If history shows us anything we have a pretty good track record of coming through. And we have some pretty awesome support people right next to us all along the metaphorical obstacle course.

Whatever it is, there's nothing too big that you won't persevere through. Surrounded by the freedom to feel authentically. Surrounded by love. Surrounded by hope. Surrounded by those who understand. Never alone. Never ever.

Stuck in Alabama Mud

I love movies. A movie full of silliness and quite fun to quote is "My Cousin Vinny." Aside from being a source of many hilarious lines, one line has always stood out to me recently as a very poignant life lesson. One of the main characters describes what it is like to have your car tires stuck in the mud.

Challenges are inevitable in life. We do, however, have a choice on how we deal with these challenges. When faced with a problem, we can either sit in the car, push the gas and spin the tires. Nothing will change; nothing will happen…except maybe digging ourselves deeper into the mud. Or we can get out of the car, walk behind it and do the dirty hard work of pushing, digging and working to make a shift.

Often, we sit and spin our wheels when we are faced with a challenge, we continue to spin, push the gas harder, yell, get frustrated and repeat the cycle over and over again. Why do we expect different results from doing the exact same thing, and then get irritated when nothing changes? Why? Change is difficult. Change is hard work. Change is vulnerable. This is why it is vital to have safe people in our lives to challenge us when we are stuck. This is why we need real friends and mentors who will call us out when we are spinning and spinning and spinning. These people don't tell us what we necessarily 'want' to hear. They challenge us with the truth. They hold us accountable; they encourage us to be our best and will get out of the car with us, end up covered in thick, icky mud to help push that car out of the rut.

No one can make the choice for us to get out of the car and do the hard work. No one can actually do all of the work for us. But we can accept and receive the help of those around us to lessen the burden of doing it alone. Let yourself be supported. When you let someone help you, you both will be changed forever. Let yourself see that you are worth receiving love and support, and not only giving these to others.

Challenges are inevitable. Defeat is optional. Let yourself be loved by those around you and help you get unstuck. Some days are "get out of the car and do the work we need to do to move forward," and some days are "stand with another to help them get unstuck." Wherever you are today, you are supported!

Love Without Expectation

I was recently asked, "what's the worst response to 'I love you?'"

I didn't understand the question. I'm not stupid, but my mind and soul couldn't comprehend why someone would ask this question. You see, if I say "I love you" to someone with an expectation of a response, then that is love with an agenda and not authentic.

So, if I am seeking a reply, that's "the worst."

Apparently, that was not the answer they wanted. They wanted justification for their anger. But it's the only answer I know. I won't say words unless I mean them. My soul doesn't understand expectations when loving others.

Once we put something into the universe we cannot take it back. If we say something because it's what someone wants to hear or with a motive, that is in direct conflict with authenticity and love. I only want true and pure energy put forth so I may be fortunate enough to be a reason someone feels seen, feels love, feels acceptance.

Strength of character is built upon the words we speak, and the actions we take. They must align. They

Lindsay Shigemoto

cannot be at odds with each other. Love in action. Words backed by action.

My goodness, loving because that's who we are, there is nothing better. Seeing someone receive that love… oh my soul rejoices.

You are love in action. You are a life changing hero. Never stop. Never change who you are. It is beautiful.

Surrender the Control

Alanis Morissette has song lyrics that examine surrender, letting go and the feeling of over-whelm.

Some days we have to let go of control one more time. The dang surrender. When we are in battle with the pause. The tug of war over our integrity. Wanting to placate self or keep our word and stay true to self. Hold steadfast and not compromise our integrity nor our character. But this forced pause often is messy. The more than we can handle part- oh self-sufficiency our old foe returned because this time the pause feels familiar.

We are often challenged with one aspect of life that tries to ooze into other areas. Trying to pull focus from truth. Trying to overwhelm. Trying to pull other foes forward. It's okay to just be okay. Okay is enough.

It is in these moments when our true self is in battle that we strengthen character, meet some old foes once again, and decide if we truly are what we claim to be. Evidence up to this point is valid, and each choice strengthens or weakens our foundation. Foundation of hope or despair?

In these moments we find what we truly are. The shift often goes from one intent of old foe, to needing to take care of self. We hit that moment of surrender, and the pause no longer has power over us. We find gratitude in the waiting. It is hard, that's the truth; but the breakthrough has to happen before we can go to the next piece. Find gratitude for those moments when we have let go of the old and are hopeful to move into something new.

Foundation of integrity. Foundation of love. Foundation of growth. Foundation of hope. The hope for ourselves will become the hope for another. The hope for one, will become the hope for many. Hope built from character.

In these moments believing that someone believes it will all be okay, is enough...until we can believe for ourselves. Experience shows us things will be okay. So, we use the data, the proof, along with all of the faith we can muster to believe in this hope.

No one expects us to have it together all of the time. And if they do? They aren't meant for us. That has to become a non-negotiable. No performing, no pretending. Because being as we are, is always enough.

When you are in a forced pause, you begin to feel that overwhelm or battle of foes creeping back in, remember what you know. You know your core truth. You know your character. You know that hope. Hope driven by love. You are a fighter. A brave and courageous warrior. You are love in human form.

Embrace Your Story

We are all created for a reason. We all have a past. We all have extremes of hard, challenging or even evil parts, along with the beautiful, easy, hopeful parts mixed with a lot of in between moments. Every experience we have had integrates and is a part of who we are. What we choose to do with these experiences is what matters.

Do we allow them to define us, dictate our actions, feed us our identity? Or do we integrate the information from lessons learned into our truest soul identity as we embrace the beautiful pure things and reject the dark, hard things. Do we learn from challenges or sit in defeat?

When we embrace the challenges as a foundation of strength, when we reject what is not love, when we integrate through the lens of hope, our true soul identity is freely expressed. When we embrace our stories, we offer hope to others.

There is no shame in who we are, where we have been, and where we are called. There is only love. Love that fosters hope, safety and vulnerability. Love that pierces the hardened heart so that another soul might remember truth.

We must never discount something we have walked through as insignificant. When we have truly accepted things as they have been, integrated the lessons, and are loving freely in our identity, the universe will send us the ones who need to hear us, the ones who need to see us, the ones who need our story. The ones who need to be heard by us, seen by us and loved by us. We only need to be prepared to answer.

Those little soul nudges? When we walk in our story with confidence, they become more frequent, they become the whispers of soul to soul, they become part of our place in someone else's life. When we show up, the universe trusts us with much.

Embrace your story. It is so valuable, so important, so relevant. You are changing lives, you are offering hope, you are an example of authenticity. Please don't ever shrink back, please don't ever allow this world to lie to you, please believe truth and remember your soul is love.

Impact

There are places that are waiting for you to arrive. Places untouched for a long time by a pure hearted loving soul. These places, and the people don't know what they long for, but they know something is on the horizon.

When you show up exactly as you are, whether in peace or the middle of a mess, trust that is exactly what is needed in those places.

Your soul, no matter what is happening around us, tells the story that needs to be told.

Your impact will continue to be felt. Leaving something in these places forever, that when someone walks where you have been, they will feel a shift. Those who have the ability to see you, feel your energy, or catch a smile will forever be changed. They might know why, or they might not....either way, they won't be able to go back to what was.

Your pure energy is hope, it is love, it is life changing. Things move when you show up. So, arrive to these places that wait expectantly for your soul exactly as you are. It is enough. And it is beautiful.

Soul Whispers

The world is loud. External forces screaming loudly at us, often overshadowing the whispers of truth. The whispers to our soul.

When we pause and quiet the loudness of the world and focus on our soul; we hear the gentle whispers, the kind words, the kindred friends sharing hope and love; and we reconnect with the good in this world.

The world screams. This world is a broken place. Often hope feels lost. Then we remember, it isn't our job to save everyone. It isn't our job to solve the world's problems. Our only job is to be the truest, most pure form of our loving, pure, tender-hearted souls. When we show up and act in alignment with just being us exactly as we are; the good, the messy, the in between, magical things happen around us. Healing happens around us. We are only responsible for showing up, not the outcome.

We just need to listen. We just need to pay attention. That person that catches our eye, that heart tug to reach out to a friend, that soul whisper to write, or paint, or dance, or make someone laugh. This is our purpose of love. We show up. We stay. We are the expression of the goodness we know exists. It's not futile. It's hard most days, but the impact we may not see is worth it for ourselves and for all of humanity.

Please be encouraged that nothing you do is futile! You are changing this world we live in one moment at a time.

Decide

We don't get much say over how or when we leave this world, but we do get to decide how we're going to live. So, do it. Decide. Is this the life path meant for me? Did I settle? Is this the life I want to live? Did I settle? Is this the best version of me? Am I settled?

Decide. Breathe in. Breathe out and decide.

Our souls already know the answers to these questions and others. Trouble is, we live in a world that's loud. So much pressure to be this, do that, conform to this, fit this mold. Expectations. Oh my, the expectations.

And when we finally come into alignment with what we know, taking action can be scary. The unknown can be scary. I sit here reminding myself that staying where I cannot be the next level of my best self is even scarier.

Are we fully committed to being our best self? Our soul knows how, with whom and where we are meant to go. It's fair to say, by now you know I will NOT live my life stagnant. My current best self is not my end best self. Always learning, always growing, always expanding. There's more to do. No pressure-only long-ing to elevate.

Decide to shift. To be in alignment with where we are called, who we are, and what we are meant to do. Decide to make some changes. Buckle up for this next level, it's going to be challenging, and will stretch us in new ways. But absolutely in full alignment with where we are called in our lives and a love for humans is reward beyond measure.

Rest and the Hustle

There are so many things I want to do and want to execute. There are so many things I want to get done. There are so many things I need to get done, the drive within me often prevents me from resting.

Busyness used to be one of my favorite addictions. My heart and soul long to do so much, but I find it hard to remember rest. Where do we find balance between the fire within our souls, and the need to take care of ourselves?

The fire within our souls is for humanity. This internal tug-of-war between knowing we need rest, knowing we need to take care of ourselves, and knowing we've been given beautiful assignments by the universe, to benefit one, and then another, the ones who need us, the ones the universe designed for us to help.

Maybe rest doesn't look like what society tells us it is. Maybe laying down is rejuvenating and not being lazy. Maybe taking a break is restoration. Maybe pausing in the overwhelm will reignite the flame to be more effective when we are beyond tired. Maybe rest doesn't have an agenda. Maybe rest is necessary.

Rest so we can hustle for humanity. People who have been gifted with big ideas and big dreams to benefit others often burn out. I don't want to be that statistic. So, we ask ourselves what can we do to prevent that burn out? What can we do today to calm our nervous systems, to restore peace, to fill our humanity hustle tanks?

Some of us often believe rest is necessary for everyone else, but not for ourselves. Perpetual uniqueness... Why are we the exception to what we believe to be so necessary for everyone else?

So, let's take a minute or a few to rest ourselves. Because we know that when we come back, we will be better. It's up to us to love ourselves enough, to believe what we believe for everyone else for ourselves, to rest enough to hustle for our assignments.

You deserve rest. You deserve restoration. You deserve self-love. Let go of the self-imposed expectations, ignore the expectations of others, because where you are today is exactly enough. No need to do, only be. Wishing you a day of whatever makes your soul at peace, a day for you to take care of yourself, a day for self-love, a day to receive love. You are enough exactly as you are.

Truth from Chaos

When things feel chaotic from change, from situations we can't control, from internal dialogue, we fight to remember truth.

The truth of who we are. The truth of who we were created to be in this world. The truth of what we know. We are love. We have been given beautiful gifts in this life for a reason.

People will hurt us. Intentionally or not, the impact is the same. It is important to remember that it isn't about us at all. Hurt people hurt people. This is why truth is so important.

The opposite is true. Healed people heal people. Free people, free people. This is our love in action. To love others so deeply because we have done the deep hard work.

Things will continue to come up. Each hard day, each feeling when we are hurt is a lesson. What can I learn, what don't I want to be, where can I improve? All under the banner of truth.

The truth that we are valued. We are enough. Our feelings are valid. We deserve love. We deserve respect. We are worthy.

Lindsay Shigemoto

When we frame things in truth, the perspective often shifts in situations. Though the world is dark, and people cause harm, it is not a reflection of us as an individual human.

It can often feel overwhelming, and hard. It's okay to be angry and sad when the world tries to push back. But we remember the truth. We are life changers. Love wins. Always.

May you never forget your worth, your value, your love. The impact your every existence has in this world is so critical, so necessary. Please don't ever forget this or let the lies of this world ever quiet the truth. May these words remind you of the truth.

Shine!

When a candle is lit it breaks through the darkness. This alone is a beautiful miracle. A single light penetrating the unknown.

What happens when that candle gives off itself and shares its light? Another flame is ignited. Then another flame, followed by another and yet another. The first singular flame's radiance doesn't dim by sharing its light.

Suddenly, the small area of light has extended to a whole room filled with light. All from one single original flame, burning no less brightly. When we shine our light on the dark and questionable things of this world, things are exposed, the hidden become seen. With every new soul that is reached by our light, the collective light grows stronger, and it will change this world.

Never be afraid of sharing your light my friend. The light you have permeates this dark world. Your light is undoubtedly igniting many more to shine brightly. I imagine if we had a view of the impact you have had on people, the illumination we would see in this world would be magical and so bright.

If you ever feel like your light is starting to fade, don't worry my friends, those who love and encourage you will never hesitate to help reignite that flame of hope within you.

Now let's go conquer this day by shining brightly. Together, one at a time, we will change this world.

Change the Trajectory

Every moment is a beginning. Everything we have achieved in life began with a decision to act. The first step. Things rarely, if ever fall into our lives. Hard work and perseverance get us to the goal but long before that was the first step.

Every life change comes with us taking action. Hitting the submit button to a job, sending off a submission to a publisher, booking the trip, or stepping into that next audition. Any of which may be the very thing that changes the trajectory of the next phase of our lives.

And when we look back, that seemingly ordinary day was anything BUT ordinary.

So today, I encourage you to decide. Make those dreams become a reality by taking that step. Change the trajectory, something out there is waiting for your YES!

Sit Down

We all have tragic parts to our stories. Details in our lives that don't shine on their own. Oh, but when we gain awareness, do the hard excavating and we learn, there is growth.

We rise up. We rise to the occasion with a history and foundation of tragedy and beauty. We rewrite the narrative.

We shift our perspective to; this is what tried to keep me from stepping into my greatest self and this is how I told it to sit down.

Lies-sit down. Self-doubt, sit down. Old patterns-sit down. False identity-sit down. World-sit down.

Truth—stand up! Self-confidence—stand up! Healed patterns—stand up! True identity—stand up! Purpose-stand up!

COME FORTH—truth, confidence, identity, purpose! This is how we make change. This is how we impact. This is how we show hope.

We tell our stories to share hope. We SHOW people their power, their truth, we show them how to make those hindering parts sit down. We show them their power! We show them how to stand up! We show them how to thrive.

There is no expectation of perfection. That's not reality. We show them how to recalibrate if there is a moment or few of old thinking. We show them how to continue. How to believe in better and not give up. We show them how they can live. It comes down to love.

Keep telling your old to sit down and the truth to stand. Keep calling forth your power. You are love in action. You are showing others their power. You are showing them hope.

Please never give up. No matter what, you will stand. We stand together. We love together. Healing this broken place one soul at a time. Never alone. Never ever. Always worthy of the I love you.

The Overwhelm

The overwhelm and the freeze. That's a recurrent struggle for many of us. Busyness addiction, a comfortable ugly foe, begins a vicious cycle. It's not that we can't or won't come out of it, it may be that we are maybe fearful of failure or even more fearful of success and we get overwhelmed and freeze.

When the overwhelm feels huge, and the complexity is our enemy; we have to remember the why. Why did we have these dreams, why did we want to start, and shift to what can we do right now, what pieces can be executed in the meantime, what piece of the purpose can happen while we tackle the seemingly daunting mountains?

We've survived difficult and challenging things, and we are still here. Why wouldn't we be able to succeed beyond survival? Success isn't to be feared. It's okay to be seen. The love for others and helping is far more important than the roadblocks. Roadblocks within our minds or those thrown up by others.

The universe always makes a way. We will know when to act, where to go, how to get there, who to bring along and who to serve.

Love in action. Motion forward. One bit at a time. There are NO little movements in working a big dream, every detail is so intricately designed. We just need to listen, to see, to feel, to pay attention and to act.

Please don't ever stop. If it's for the one, then that is exactly enough. Keep moving forward. You have all the love and support from those around you moving toward your dream.

Reflection of Purpose

I am sitting here this morning reflecting with the sounds of the mighty Pacific Ocean as my soundtrack.

The Spotted Comb Jellyfish (Leucothea Pulchra), this beautiful creature, exists. As I studied this vision of existence it felt like time stood still. I knew there was a lesson. So, I stayed. The longer I stayed watching, the more I felt. The more I learned. Not about this animal, but about all of us.

What is this animal's purpose? I didn't know. The questions came to me…is that important information in order for me to appreciate and celebrate what I see before me? Is it for me to figure out? Will it continue its purpose without my opinions?

The lesson wasn't about the beauty at all. It's for all of humanity. It's not my job to determine, comment on, or understand another's purpose. My only job is love so deeply that my fellows can thrive on their journey. Love deeply, share encouraging words, and be a reminder to them that only they can fulfill their divine purpose here. No one else needs to understand it for it to be true.

My goodness. If we take time to reconnect with nature, she never disappoints. Nothing is insignificant. Everything, everyone has a purpose. It may be that no one else sees, understands or supports this, but none of that matters. The creator knows why we are here.

It just takes some remembering on our part sometimes.

What We Nourish Will Flourish

What are we choosing to feed?

Challenging days are inevitable. What we do have control over is how we respond. Our previous experiences and the work we have done through them are the foundation up to any point of difficulty. The work we continue to do through it and remembering how we have walked through challenges before are all groundwork for progress and expansion.

We must acknowledge and honor our emotions and not shove them down. There is a difference between avoidance and using tools to work through. The latter honors us. It leads to growth. The emotions and hard or challenging circumstances are not our focus, but they are a lesson. We are always learning, growing and elevating.

I encourage you, when you find yourself in a challenging or difficult situation, to nourish the growth, nourish the gratitude, and nourish the hope of a better future. Gratitude shifts perspective and this is where we can remind ourselves of how far we have come and look forward with hope and excitement.

So proud of you! Keep up the work of being yourself. It's a beautiful existence.

Don't Make Me Buy You Groceries

I had a conversation with a friend who was doing a whole lot of life. As the situation was, she was traveling for work, a new city every week, and eating what she could grab. I said to her, "Don't make me buy you groceries."

I want my life to be remembered for actions like this. The "Don't make me buy you groceries," moments. Love in action. I don't believe in empty words.

One day when my time in this world is over, I want people to go out and love hard on people in honor of my legacy (well, I want this every day now, really). I want people who know me to love others when they are missing me. I want the humans in my life to share the ginormous soul hug with someone when I am not there to offer them one. I want them to bake something special for another person because I would. I want them to make others laugh at simple silly things. I want them to offer words of encouragement and hope as I would. I want my life to be remembered for loving others deeply. For the kind of love that is seemingly uncommon. For the kind of love that I live every day trying to make known to humanity. For the kind of love that reminds us that goodness exists. For the kind of love that makes me weird. I'll take weird. I'll take different. I'll take it because it is my purpose to love deeply.

So, every day I love as hard and as deeply as I can. While I can. Maybe, just maybe when my time here in this world is finished, the ripple of my life won't stop. Maybe, just maybe, my legacy will be this one of deeply rooted love. Love without expectation, without performance, without needing to be earned. Love simply based on existing.

So today, this week, let's love others deeply. Whatever that looks like. We will know the who and the what. Sometimes it is a smile, sometimes it is encouragement, sometimes it is laughter (one of my favorites), sometimes it is all of these things. We know. We will always know.

You deserve all of the grocery love threats, all of the laughter, all of the love and goodness in this world. You are worthy and valued beyond your comprehension. Never forget these important truths…and if you do? I'll be here to help you remember.

Your Next

In life we have choices. From spur of the moment, to potentially life changing decisions. When I look forward, I see a series of thoughtful decisions. Choices of what's next. Different paths leading different places. And all so beautiful. The larger picture, but so deeply intimate for each one.

The challenges and trials we face in life are often against seemingly impossible odds. Acknowledging that life can often be difficult, and through it all focusing on love. On what makes us happy. Seeking joy in each moment. Striving for better days even when it hurts to breathe.

It is your belief in something bigger. It is your belief in better. It is your perseverance. It is your courage, your hope, your redemption story, your legacy. Because how do we measure the value of our lives? Not by material things, financial successes, business ventures, professional accomplishments, but rather by love. Not to accumulate for ourselves or checking off a box. Rather by loving others, we become fulfilled. It is our heartbeat. It is our very being. Our increments of love toward and for others, is our measure.

Perseverance. Courage. Kindness. Hope. Love.

This is your next. This is your life story. How will you write it?

Let Your Words Enslave No One

I recently had someone say something to me that was the opposite of hope and encouragement. It was full of harmful intent.

Words have power to speak life or cause harm. How do we want to be remembered? We cannot control words spoken to us, but we can choose to accept or reject them. It has taken me many years to realize this (and I certainly do not have this mastered yet…we are all works in progress).

Sometimes words hit like a roundhouse kick to the gut. After I catch my breath, I have to refocus and think, "What is the truth?" I have a choice each time. I can say "I receive that," and allow it to integrate into my being, or I can say, "I do not receive that," and reject the lies and hate, banishing them far away.

How do you want to be remembered? As one with words like daggers? Or as one with words like salve?

I started thinking of a quote I saw recently that discussed speaking to others as if it was your last time speaking with them. So powerful.

Why wait? Say the important things now. Tell people what they mean to you. Let them know how they

Lindsay Shigemoto

have inspired your life. Remind them of their value, their importance, their impact.

Words matter. The intent of words matters. Use your words to enslave no one. Use your words to spark hope. Use your words to give life. Use your words to heal. Use your words to encourage. Let your words be your legacy.

I hope my own legacy is one of love.

White Noise

Busyness. We've all been there. Commitments, desires, responsibilities, and the list goes on, leading us to blocked calendars, leading us to pressure and anxiety to get it all in…leading us to burn out.

Busyness. Somewhere along the way it has become a badge of honor people wear. It has become an idol. The comparison of busy. In our society we sit around talking about ALL the things (eye roll) we have to do in our days as if it somehow gives us value. I refuse to compare busyness with others because it serves no healthy purpose.

I had a mentor years ago suggest I clear my entire calendar (except work, spouse, and child commitments) because I was depleted. So much white noise. So many scheduled activities that were there only to fill space. My initial knee jerk reaction was "absolutely not." The "doer" in me was at battle with the idea of just "being." But wait, hadn't I asked for guidance? So, I did as she asked and really took a look at why I reacted the way I did. Busyness was a way to avoid. Busyness had become my addiction. Doing had become my identity. Busyness…because rest was unfamiliar.

I have found that what I fill my time with can either be life giving or life draining. My schedule does not give me value. Busyness is not my identity. Doing is not my identity. My value comes from my purpose, for me, that purpose is love. BE-ing my authentic self…love. So today, I choose to fill my time with life giving, green light activities and less white noise busyness. When I am "being" myself, the "doer" is also content.

Less white noise, more life-giving choices. My schedule often looks busier than before, yet, every day, I am given the abundant energy I need to be of service to my fellows. For that is my purpose here. Busyness will NOT be my idol.

If you find yourself depleted, or in a time of necessary BE-ing when your history is of DO-ing, I encourage you to take a moment or a few to ask yourself, am I filled by white noise or life-giving activities. It may be time for white noise decluttering. Then make the change that feels authentic for you.

You'll know. You always know.

Remembering and Legacy

This morning, I woke up wondering what one of my favorite aunts, Joan, would have been doing. Maybe training others somewhere across the nation on IEPs and rights for disabled children. Maybe, today would have been a day she got to spend with some students, being the voice to the voiceless. Or maybe, today would have been a quiet day at home, waiting for all of her family to come to visit and spend the weekend together. But that isn't what her Facebook status said. Instead, it is an active account that hasn't been touched since October 23, 2012.

Today, if she could post from heaven, I imagine it might say something like this:

October 23, 2023: It has been 11 years my family has been navigating that thing we called life, without me. What has become of my legacy? That of a daughter, a wife, a mother, an aunt, a sister, a friend, and a special needs advocate cut short because a criminal made the active decision to drive a big rig while impaired.

What lives on for me? My children, my nieces and nephews, my forgiveness and my love. I do not suffer here. To those who love me, there is no need to suffer for me. Choose to LIVE for me. Choose to LOVE for me.

Do not let your remembrance of me be my passing, rather; advocate, love deeply, experience life as I did. Be my legacy. Be the hope for others. Be the reason others believe in better.

I do not suffer here, please, though it may be difficult on some days, do not suffer for me. Remember me, share pieces of me with those you meet; sprinkle my love to those you meet, so you build your own legacy.

What's your legacy? How will you be remembered? Go out and live that big, beautiful life now for we are not guaranteed tomorrow.

Right Foot Brave Left Foot Courage

W e all need reminders. Reminders of truth, reminders of hope, reminders of growth, reminders of worth, reminders of perseverance, and reminders of love.

We have all lived and survived various things in our time here. Some pleasant, some not. I am not a fan of the phrase, "Everything happens for a reason," but that is a discussion for another time. Sometimes the "not times" have no reason other than evil. However, the fight to heal, grow, persevere, and thrive often speak louder than the situations one has endured. We can look back and see and believe in our purposes. The beauty of our existence, the survivors, the fighters. The brave warriors. All of this is the reasoning behind the meaning of my feet tattoos.

Right foot brave left foot courage. A reminder for me, those who see and ask about them, for those who know me, for those I will meet; the reminder to walk each step of every day with bravery and courageousness. Some barefoot days I will get a quick glance at my feet with those words and am in awe of my life and the lives of those around me. We are still here.

No one else gets to define what is brave and coura-
geous for you. You decide. You take the actions. That's
the key, action. One step at a time. Right foot brave left
foot courage.

No matter what has been thrown at us in this life,
no matter what comes up next, we can remember these
truths. That we are indeed brave, that being present and
showing up takes courage. Your actions impact those
around you. Actions spark inspiration and that is a form
of love. There is nothing, absolutely nothing, that can
overcome or defeat love. Love wins. Always.

The Long Road

One of my favorite moments in the musical "Hadestown" is within the song called Wait for Me (Reprise). This number contains so many powerful words. One of my favorite pieces of this number is when Hermes speaks to Orpheus. Hermes is warning Orpheus that the battle is not the task at hand, but that which resides in his own mind.

Oof. I certainly relate, I imagine we all have felt the battle within ourselves at some point in time.

Life is challenging. Period. If life was easy, there would be no growth. And no one ever told us growth was comfortable or painless.

I encourage you all to go and read the song, or even better go listen. The battle is often within ourselves. The self-doubt, the doubt from others we have unconsciously filed away, that surfaces in times of challenge or opportunity, the battle lies within. So, what can we do?

We create reminders of truth. What do we know to be true? What evidence from previous experiences supports my growth, my abilities, my character? Who in my life can help me remember? Who can I ask for support in this moment?

No matter what you are facing, whether personal growth or challenge, or professional growth or opportunity, you are never walking alone. Please do not let the battle within your mind take hold. Someone somewhere out there is rooting for you. Cheering you on. Loving you through the process. Ready to speak words of truth and love back into your reality.

The long road doesn't have to be the lonely one. Challenges will come, but it does not have to be the path to ruin, you can reach the path to Paradise and your next dream. And I know, you won't have to look too far to find the ones who walk with you, who stand with you, who fight with you.

Art and Artist

I love art. In any form. Paintings, written word, dance, theater, music, all of it. Art is meant to evoke emotion. I have no interest in "experts" telling me the "correct" interpretation; to me that defeats the purpose of art. Everyone lives with different experiences and will witness something different. That IS the beauty. That is the purpose of art. It prompts discussion, it creates community, it is love.

In college I studied art history for fun. It was my passion class. I have my favorite pieces by various artists, but one piece caused me to feel emotions so deeply that I could not dismiss its place in my life. It quickly became my favorite Picasso, "Girl Before a Mirror."

When I studied this in college, I saw her having such a disdain for her reflection (insert my projection of self in this interpretation), so when I saw it in person recently, not only was I in love with it even more, but something had shifted. I hardly recognize the girl who thought that way of initial interpretation. Now I see such adoration and self-love I could not see before. A compassion, an appreciation. A deep, pure love.

Lindsay Shigemoto

The beauty of art. Shifting. Evolving. Healing. Growth. Never one interpretation. Art is a reflection not only of the artist but of the audience.

We are both art and artists. Created to love, created to express, created for purpose. What will you create with your life? What will you leave here to impact others? What emotions will you evoke in others?

Does your interpretation of you as a work of art need to change? Has it already? And as an artist, what masterpieces will you leave as your legacy?

Though the "Girl Before a Mirror" has not changed since its completion, I have. And now, I continue on this journey called life with my own art; hopefully impacting others deeply the way this piece impacted and continues to impact me and my purpose.

Redefine Brave

Brave: adjective: having or showing courage. Synonymous with courageous, fearless, heroic. Antonymous with coward, weakhearted, fearful.

Sure, that is how Merriam-Webster defines brave; but WHAT EXACTLY DOES THAT MEAN? Does bravery look the same for everyone? Does it have to? Do only awful things make someone brave? What are the standards for what is brave and what isn't? I think it is time we redefine brave.

Imagine a little girl who survived the most unspeakable acts as a child, who went through life toughing it out, with a smile on her face. She is called brave, strong, courageous, and a hero by others. But to her it wasn't brave, it wasn't courageous, it was the only way to survive because it wasn't a choice. She doesn't equate survival with bravery, but she is repeatedly told that she is strong and brave, so that eventually she starts to believe that suffering in silence equals strength equals brave, so she lives a life of suffering.

Imagine a little boy bullied on the playground, never shedding a tear. Smiling and trying to hide the pain inside. Day after day, mean hateful words penetrating his soul, all while smiling and trying to say the right thing or act the "right way" pretending it doesn't hurt him. They say he is a strong boy and a hero because he doesn't cave to bullies, he knows who he is, and they can't beat him down. He is brave. But this isn't his choice. It is survival. He knows he will get beat up if he fights back, so he suffers in silence, because silence equals strength equals brave, so he lives a life of suffering.

What if we redefine brave to what is hardest for each of us. What if it isn't a blanket term that has certain parameters? What if it is simpler than that? What if we listen to what our souls and hearts are afraid of most, and we conquer that fear...what if that is our brave?

What if suffering in silence, being the "good girl" or "good boy," and not speaking up is how brave was defined for you? What if your brave is admitting you need help, admitting you aren't as strong as you make it seem, admitting that you are suffering in a situation, asking for the help and then receiving the help. What if your brave is taking care of yourself?

What if you got to redefine your brave? What would that look like? Would you apply for the job you secretly wanted? Would you speak up to the bully that shattered your dignity? Would you surrender your control and accept the love of others without fear? Would you paint that canvas without expectation? Would you step back into an audition room one more time? Would you write that book you always wanted to write? What is your, "what would I?"

You already know the answer. Believe in yourself. Honor your soul. Honor your knowing. Redefine brave. You get to choose. Those other things that others see as being brave are true to them, they may see you as a hero, and that is inspiring…that gives people hope. It is okay to let others call you these things, but real bravery is individual. What you choose. You get to choose what your brave looks like. And does it really matter if anyone else understands? Those that honor you and respect the real you will see your "brave." They will support you and help you do the thing you fear most. They will help you redefine brave. It likely will not be an easy task. In fact, confronting or admitting what we fear is icky and hard. But you can do it, you will do it, and it will be worth it.

Go out there and let us each redefine brave. Lift each other up, be kind to each other, and honor each other's brave. You can do this!! You are so worth it, and you are loved.

Happenstance

Coincidences. Happenstance. Happy accidents. Random meetings. Chance. We have all heard these explanations. I don't believe in those terms. I like to envision and believe that these moments are part of a divinely choreographed dance in this life.

We all know those moments. The prompting to ask a question, which is the springboard in finding another soul friend. The gentle nudge to say hello to a new person only to find out they are friends with your own dear friend. The people who live across the country but are in the same vacation city as you when you strike up a conversation, you find out one of them is headed to college in your neighboring town. The human who hired you, only to find out that their precious family member works closely with one of your beloved family members.

We are meant to be relational creatures. Seeking moments to find the connections with others is one of my favorite things, because I love loving people. I love to celebrate differences, and find commonalities, I love to learn from others in ways I have not known. When we seek to truly know another, we find these soul strings connecting us together.

When the world feels so large and often intimidating, I encourage each of you to find the strings of connection. The connections that cannot be explained by "chance." The reminders that in this seemingly large intimidating world, if we seek opportunities and people, we find out that this world is actually very small and beautifully intimate.

May you find the strings of connection. May you freely experience your divinely choreographed dance with those meant for you. All you have to do is listen to your soul and take that first step. You will know. You will always know.

Why Wait?

I was once asked "Have you written your letters for your loved ones for when you die?" I looked at the person in shock, "Um, what?"

My spirit and soul were completely and immediately disturbed.

Why would I wait? Why would I write one letter rather than telling my loved ones these things as often as I can while I am still here?

Why would I pass up an opportunity to remind someone of their value, their worth, their impact.

Why would I wait to tell them how much they are loved, how important they are to me, and how they have changed my life?

Why would I withhold opportunities to see a smile, witness a spark of confidence, experience a beautiful shift because I spoke the truth?

Why would I ration words of hope, love, and encouragement meant to be shared with someone?

Why would I hoard these things until I die?

Why wouldn't I take every chance I have to speak words of life to another?

I know so little in this vast world of ours, but I know this to be true; speaking life, telling others you believe in them, what you see they can achieve, offering hope, giving encouragement, sharing what you admire, what you appreciate, and how they have changed you for the better IS the legacy. Not some memorialized words on a page.

The experienced impact. The integration of the words and actions. The vast ripple effect. Not a written legacy love letter. A living legacy of love. That's what I aim for. That's my mission.

But all I could muster in the moment of response were the words, "Why wait?"

I was given a beautiful gift today from a dear friend (the day I am writing this) that it matters. My relentless belief, unwavering support, and unconditional love made an impact in her life. And I thought about the question I was asked months earlier. It mattered.

So, I offer this: Speak them now. Share them now. Act now. Change lives now. Let your legacy begin now.

Legacy love letter when my time is up? No thank you. I think I will leave a living legacy; written every precious day I have left instead. Each soul I have had the opportunity to impact *is* my legacy love letter.

Why wait?

ABOUT THE AUTHOR

Lindsay is not your average author. She is a former Doctor of Chiropractic, though her passions have always been within the arts. Her heartbeat is helping others. She loves encouraging and helping humans achieve their fullest potential. When she is not busy writing, painting, or elevating others, she can be found spending time with her family and enjoying various types of art, especially musical theater.